STEEL

Andrew Langley

Consultants: British Steel plc

Wayland

Titles in this series

Bricks	Plastics
Glass	Steel
Oil	Water
Paper	Wood

Cover: (Main picture) Molten steel is released into moulds at a steelworks in China. (Top right) Gear wheels are made of a special kind of steel.

Editor: Sarah Doughty

First published in 1992 by
Wayland (Publishers) Ltd
61 Western Road, Hove
East Sussex, BN3 1JD, England

British Library Cataloguing in Publication Data
Langley, Andrew
  Steel.—(Links)
  I. Title   II. Series
  669.1

ISBN 0 7502 0324 2

Typeset by Dorchester Typesetting Group Ltd
Printed in Italy by G. Canale & C.S.p.A.

Contents

The marvellous metal   4

Iron and steel   6

The story of steel   8

Mining the ore   10

Making iron   12

Basic oxygen process   14

Electric arc process   16

Shaping and casting   18

Using steel   20

The steelmakers   22

From old to new   24

The environment   26

Projects with steel   28

Glossary   30

Books to read   31

Index   32

All the words that appear in
bold are explained in the
glossary on page 30.

The marvellous metal

Steel is the most important metal in the world. It is made from iron, which is plentiful. Steel is cheap to make and shape, and very strong.

Our homes are filled with steel objects. Refrigerators, cookers, knives, forks, baths, sinks and radiators all have steel in them. Our tables and chairs are held together by steel nails and screws. Our clothes were probably sewn together using steel needles.

Steel is a metal that provides a strong framework for a building structure. This is the Pompidou Centre in Paris, France.

The world outside would also look very different without steel. It is used to build giant skyscrapers, bridges and oil tankers. Cars, lorries and aircraft have many steel parts. Trains run along steel rails, and steel **pylons** carry electricity cables.

Steel machines and tools are used to make many other things. They crush stone and lay roads. They cut timber and turn it into paper. They mould glass and plastic. Steel machines even printed this book!

This river barrage is made of steel and is used to stop flooding in the River Thames in London, Britain.

Iron and steel

The red streaks show that there is iron ore in this rock.

Iron is an **element**, one of the basic chemical substances. It is the world's most common element, although most of it lies in the centre of the Earth and cannot be reached.

But there is also a large amount of iron in the Earth's crust, or outer layer. Pure iron is never found by itself. It occurs as an **ore**, mixed with other elements. The ore is purified to produce iron, but this iron still contains too much of another element – **carbon**. So it is purified again, until only a little carbon remains. It is now steel.

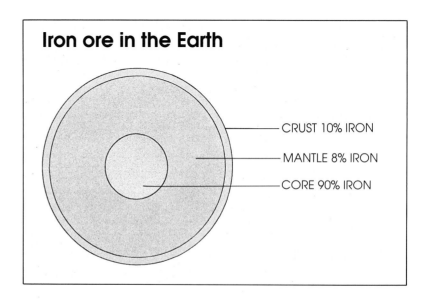

Iron ore in the Earth

CRUST 10% IRON

MANTLE 8% IRON

CORE 90% IRON

This diagram shows how much iron ore there is in the Earth.

Steel is much stronger than iron. There are many kinds of steel and they all have different uses. A hammer head must be heavy and hard. A saw blade must be flexible and sharp. A drill bit has to be very tough and able to withstand great heat. Each is made from a different type of steel.

Steel is easy to shape. It can be moulded, hammered or rolled. It can also be mixed or coated with other metals.

Molten iron pours out of a furnace at a steelworks in Australia.

The story of steel

Long ago, people found strange lumps lying on the ground. These were **meteorites**, which had fallen from space. They were made of an unknown metal. The people called it iron, which meant 'metal from the sky'.

Iron was also found as iron ore under the ground. In about 1400 BC the Hittite people (from the land which is now Turkey) discovered how to get pure metal from the ore by heating it. Pure iron made strong, sharp weapons and tools. The knowledge spread across the world, to China and Europe, beginning the period of history now called the Iron Age.

Solid iron can sometimes be found in meteorites that fall from the sky and land on Earth.

A few ironworkers found that, by heating iron on burning **charcoal** and hammering it, they could make an even tougher metal. This was steel. But it was not until 1740 that Benjamin Huntsman invented a new way of making steel, in a container called a **crucible**.

In 1856 Henry Bessemer made the first steelmaking **converter**. This could produce steel cheaply by converting it from **molten** iron in large quantities.

Henry Bessemer's converter was the first method of producing steel cheaply from molten iron.

Mining the ore

There are two ways of getting iron ore out of the ground. These methods are open-cast mining and underground mining.

Open-cast mines are used to obtain iron ore that is near the surface. Machines scrape away the top layers of soil and rocks. The ore beneath is broken up with explosive charges. Then mechanical diggers take away the pieces.

An open-cast mine in Western Australia. The iron ore that is found underground lies near the surface.

Some ore lies much deeper underground. Miners dig tunnels down into the ore and break it up. The pieces are hoisted out of the tunnel in buckets, and taken away on conveyor belts or in railway trucks.

Cargo ships or trains carry the ore to a stockyard. Here the large pieces of ore are crushed to the size of a snooker ball. These smaller pieces are mixed with **coke** and heated to form a mixture called **sinter**. This is now ready to be made into iron.

A train carrying iron ore waits to leave the mine in Wyoming, USA to go to a stockyard.

Making iron

A steelworker draws off the molten iron from the blast furnace.

A blast furnace extracts the iron from the ore. The furnace is a tall tower lined with fire bricks. A mixture of sinter, coke and **limestone** is loaded into the top of the furnace. The mixture is let down inside the furnace through a special **valve**. The valve stops gases and heat from escaping.

Very hot air is blown in through pipes at the bottom of the furnace. This quickly makes the mixture white hot. The heat from the burning coke melts the iron. The limestone combines with the rock and other material in the ore. It rises to the top of the melted iron and forms a scum called **slag**. The molten iron falls to the hearth at the bottom of the furnace.

The blast furnace keeps working day and night. The iron is drawn off through a hole near the bottom, and the slag through another hole higher up. More iron ore mixture is added at the top.

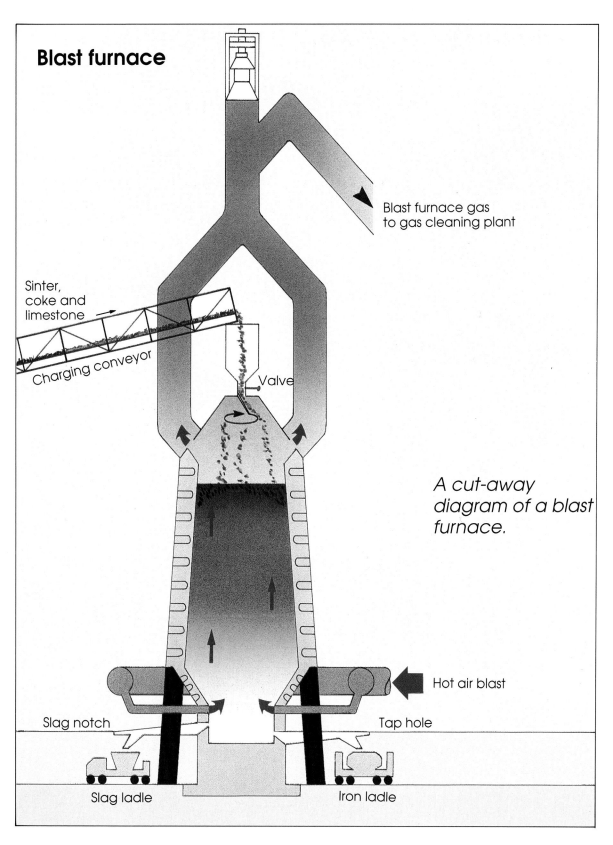

Blast furnace

Sinter, coke and limestone

Charging conveyor

Valve

Blast furnace gas to gas cleaning plant

A cut-away diagram of a blast furnace.

Hot air blast

Slag notch

Tap hole

Slag ladle

Iron ladle

Basic oxygen process

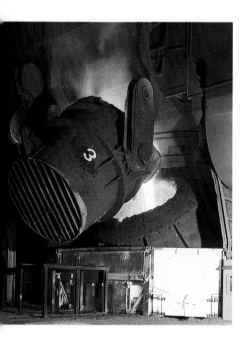

Today, most iron is used to make steel. The hot metal goes directly from the blast furnace into the steelmaking plant. There are two methods – the main method is the basic **oxygen** process. The second method – the electric arc process – is used to make special steels.

Molten iron is poured into the basic oxygen furnace.

The basic oxygen process is cheap and fast. It is the most important modern way of producing steel. The steelmaking furnace is shaped like a giant concrete-mixer, which can be tipped to either side. Steel scrap is put into the tipped-up furnace, and the molten iron is poured in.

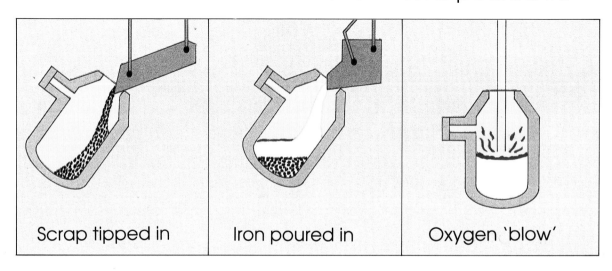

| Scrap tipped in | Iron poured in | Oxygen 'blow' |

The furnace is then turned to its upright position again.

A tube called a lance is pushed down into the metal. It sends out a blast of pure oxygen, a gas that causes very hot things to burn. Because the metal is white hot, most **impurities** immediately burn up. Some lime is added, which turns the remaining impurities into slag.

After the oxygen blast, the furnace is tipped and a sample is taken to check the quality and temperature of the steel. The furnace is then tilted so the purified steel can be poured out. Finally, the furnace is turned upside down to remove the slag.

This diagram shows the stages of making steel using the basic oxygen process, the most common method of steelmaking.

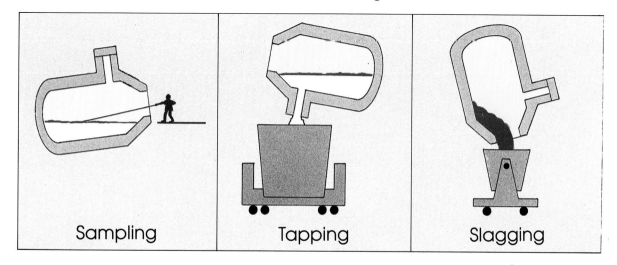

Sampling   Tapping   Slagging

Electric arc process

Hot, molten iron is not needed for the electric arc process, so cold and scrap metals are used. The process is important for making special steels, and mixes of steel with other metals. These are called **alloy** steels.

The electric arc furnace is like a huge saucepan. Its lid is lifted up, and scrap metal is tipped in. The lid is shut again. Three rods, called **electrodes**, are lowered through holes in the lid. The electricity is switched on and a powerful spark jumps between the electrodes and the metal. It produces a great heat that melts the metal.

This diagram shows the stages of making steel by the electric arc process. This process can make special and alloy steels.

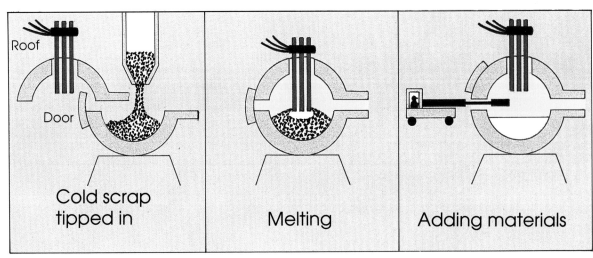

Roof

Door

Cold scrap tipped in

Melting

Adding materials

Next, lime and other materials are put into the furnace. They join with the impurities to form slag. When the process is finished, the furnace is tipped to pour off the slag. Then it is tipped the other way to pour off the steel. This is carried away in a giant bucket hung from an overhead crane.

In the electric arc furnace, an electric current flows which melts the scrap metal very quickly.

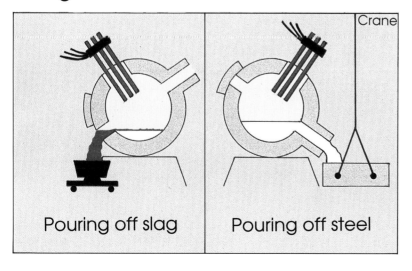

Crane

Pouring off slag | Pouring off steel

Shaping and casting

Some of the molten steel goes straight into moulds. The steel cools and hardens into slabs, called **ingots**. Later, the ingots are again heated and rolled or hammered into shape.

Most steel is shaped by a process called continuous casting. This is quicker and cheaper than the ingot process.

On the continuous casting line, the steel is squeezed between heavy rollers which press it into thin bars.

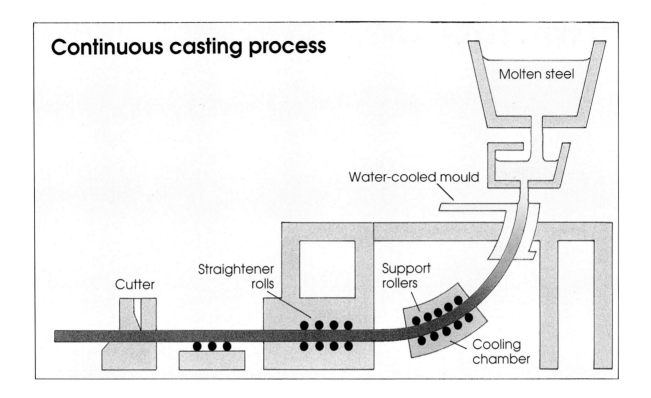

Continuous casting process

Molten steel

Water-cooled mould

Straightener rolls

Cutter

Support rollers

Cooling chamber

On the continuous casting line, the hot metal flows down through a mould, which is cooled by water. From there, the metal passes between a set of rollers. Cold water is sprayed on, hardening the steel as it moves. Finally, the hardened steel is cut into lengths.

A diagram showing how the continuous casting process works to make bars or slabs of steel.

The lengths of new steel are still not finished. They may be rolled between heavy rollers into strips or bars. They may be heated again, and then hammered into different shapes. This is called forging.

Using steel

Steel has thousands of different uses. Special kinds of steel are made to suit each job.

Carbon steel is the most useful type of steel. It is a mixture of iron and a carefully measured amount of carbon. The hardest carbon steel contains about one per cent of carbon. It is used to make tools and springs. Steel with very little carbon is the softest. It is used for car bodies and metal cans.

Many kitchen implements are made of stainless steel.

Left Most iron and steel will rust if exposed to air or water.

Below Steel pylons will not rust because they are protected by a coat of zinc.

Steel can also be mixed into alloys, with other elements, to make it stronger or more hardwearing. But it has one big problem – steel goes rusty. If **chromium** is mixed with the steel, it will not rust. The alloy made from chromium and steel is called stainless steel. Many things are made of stainless steel, from space rockets and milk tanks to spoons and razor blades.

Some types of steel are protected by a layer of plastic or another metal. Food cans are coated with **tin**. A coating of **zinc** protects electricity pylons.

The steelmakers

Steelmakers throughout the world make many millions of tonnes of steel every year. Millions of people mine and process iron ore, and millions more work in **steel mills**. Steel is one of the world's most vital products. Where does it all come from?

The USSR is the world's biggest steelmaker. It mines more iron ore than any other country, mostly for steelmaking. The USSR produces about a quarter of all the steel made in the world each year.

A steel mill in China. China is now the world's fourth largest producer of steel.

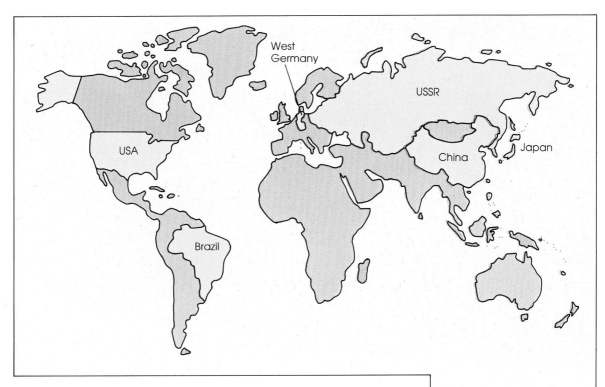

1988	Millions of tonnes
USSR	164
Japan	106
USA	91
China	59
West Germany	41
Brazil	24

Japan and the USA also make a lot of steel. But they do not have enough iron ore of the right quality (Japan has none at all). They have to buy their ore from other places, such as Australia and South America.

Other countries used to buy all their steel from Europe and the USA. Today, many have their own steel mills. The most important are in China, Brazil, Mexico and South Korea. Venezuela has the richest of all iron ore deposits, a mountain made almost entirely of iron!

A map showing which countries in the world are the major steel producers.

From old to new

A car manufacturing plant. Many of the metal parts are made of recycled materials.

Have you got a new car? It is not completely new as a lot of the metal parts have been made from recycled materials. About 40 per cent of the iron and steel has been used before – some in other cars. So there could be part of an old car inside your new one!

Old or scrap steel is vital to today's steelmakers. Scrap steel is the second most important raw material for steelmaking, after iron ore. All new steel contains some scrap. The electric arc process, as we have seen, uses nothing else.

Much of the scrap comes from worn-out vehicles, machines and buildings, as well as old metal cans and containers. Waste pieces of steel from factories and mills are also used.

First, the scrap is cleaned to get rid of unwanted rubbish. Plastic and rubber coatings are burned off. Then the scrap is broken up, and the iron is separated from the other metals.

Old, worn out vehicles in a scrap yard. Iron is separated from other metals and eventually ends up in the steelmaking furnace.

The environment

People who make and use steel have to take care to avoid damaging the world around us.

The steel industry uses up large amounts of resources. Most of the iron ore used to make steel comes from open-cast mines. These mines can spoil huge areas of land. Today most mining companies repair the sites when they have finished taking ore from the ground. They fill in the holes and replant grass and trees.

Modern steel mills have to be as efficient as possible to stop fumes and gases polluting the atmosphere.

Steelmakers also have to make sure that they do not cause pollution from fumes and gases produced as part of the steelmaking process. Modern steel mills are very efficient. The fumes that come from heating the metal are collected in a hood above the furnace. Other gases are used again as fuel for heating.

Empty steel drums that have been carelessly dumped can spoil the look of the landscape.

Steelmaking can also help our environment. The slag formed during steelmaking can be used again. Some farmers spread slag on to their fields to add lime to their soils. Slag is also used by builders who mix it with concrete to make breeze blocks (these are lightweight building blocks).

Projects with steel

Find out about rusting

You will need:

A bowl of water
A small piece of wire wool
A galvanized nail or screw

A stainless steel teaspoon
A copper coin
A small piece of aluminium foil

1. Put all the objects into a bowl of water and leave them overnight to soak.

2. Look at the objects in the bowl the next day. What do you notice about them?

You should see that the wire wool has begun to rust. This is because it is made of ordinary steel. The iron in the steel joins with the oxygen in the water to make rust.

The other objects stay the same. The nail or screw is protected by a coating of zinc. The chromium in the teaspoon joins with the oxygen in the water to form a layer which protects the steel from rusting. The coin is made from copper and nickel – metals that do not rust (although copper will slowly turn green). Aluminium does not rust either.

Make a simple compass

You will need:

A magnet
A steel needle
A cork

A saucer of water
A sharp knife

1. Cut a slice about 2 cm thick from the end of the cork. Be very careful with the knife – you should ask an adult to help you.

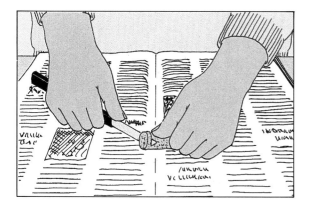

2. Hold the needle and stroke it with one end of the magnet. Stroke the needle ten times, always in the same direction and using the same end of the magnet. In this way, you magnetize the needle.

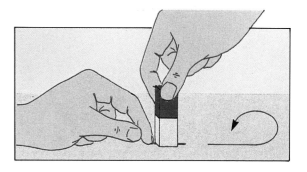

3. Push the needle right through the slice of cork, from edge to edge. Again, be very careful, and ask an adult to help you.

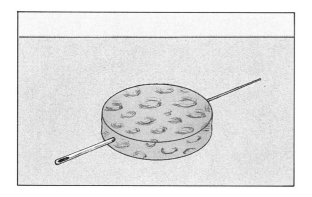

4. Place the cork very gently on the water in the saucer so that it floats. It will move around until one end points north.

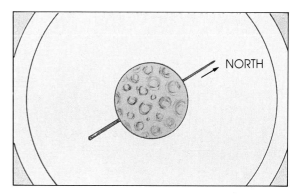

Whichever way you turn the cork, the needle will always go back to pointing north.

Glossary

Alloy   A mixture of a metal with other metals or elements.

Carbon   An element which occurs in many different forms.

Charcoal   One form of carbon. It is made by heating wood until it turns black and crumbly.

Chromium   A metallic ore which, when refined, is used to make stainless steel.

Coke   Another form of carbon. It is made by heating coal.

Converter   A furnace which converts molten iron into steel.

Crucible   A container made of a material that resists heat, used in making some special steel and alloys.

Electrodes   The two terminals (ends) of an electric cell, which conduct an electric charge.

Element   One of the basic chemical substances.

Impurities   Unwanted matter, such as dirt and rocks.

Ingot   An oblong slab of metal cast from molten steel.

Limestone   A type of rock, rich in calcium and carbon.

Meteorite   A lump of matter, usually containing metals, which lands on Earth from space.

Molten   The condition of a metal when it is very hot and melted into liquid form.

Ore   A type of rock containing metals joined with other substances.

Oxygen   An element, usually found as a gas.

Pylons   Tower-like structures made of steel, which carry electricity cables high above the ground.

Sinter   A mixture of iron ore, coke and limestone, roasted together.

Slag   A mixture of substances formed by impurities extracted during ironmaking or steelmaking.

Steel mill   A factory where steel is processed and steel objects are made.

Tin   A silvery metal, used to coat other metals to prevent them from rusting.

Valve   A hole which can be opened and closed to control the flow of materials.

Zinc   A metal often used to protect other metals from rusting.

Books to read

Burne, G. **Iron and Steel** (Wayland, 1984)
Dineen, J. **Metals and Minerals** (Young
Library, 1988)
Kerrod, R. **Metals** (Macdonald, 1981)
Lambert, M. **Focus on Iron and Steel**
(Wayland, 1987)
Langley, A. **Modern Metals** (Wayland, 1980)
Radford, D. **Looking at Metals** (Batsford,
1985)

Useful addresses

UK
Information Services
British Steel plc
9 Albert Embankment
London
SE1 7SN

USA
American Iron and Steel Institute
1000 16th Street North West
New York
20036

Sources of information
Iron and steelworks are not usually open to the public, but by writing to them
directly you may be able to organize school visits.

A number of museums present good exhibitions showing the development of
industries such as iron and steel which include models and film shows. The
Science Museum in London has a permanent exhibition of iron and
steelmaking, and towns in iron and steelmaking districts may have exhibitions
that are of some interest.

Index

Australia 7, 10, 23

basic oxygen
   process 14, 15
Bessemer, Henry 9
blast furnace 12, 13,
   14
Brazil 23

carbon 6
charcoal 9
China 8, 23
chromium 21
coke 11, 12
continuous casting
   18, 19
copper 28

Earth 6
electric arc process
   14, 16, 17, 24
Europe 8, 23

forging 19

Huntsman, Benjamin
   9

ingots 18
iron 4, 6, 7, 8, 9, 11,
   12, 14, 16, 20, 24,
   25, 28
   ore 10, 11, 12, 22,
   23, 24, 25
   oxide 6
Iron Age 8

Japan 23

magnet 29
meteorites 8
Mexico 23
mining 10, 22
   open-cast 10, 26
   underground 10

pollution 26, 27
Pompidou Centre 4

recycling 24
rusting 21, 28

sinter 11, 12
slag 12, 15, 17, 27
South America 23
South Korea 23
steel
   alloy 16, 21
   mills 22, 23, 25, 27
   scrap 14, 16, 24, 25
   stainless 20, 21

Thames barrier 5
tin 21
Turkey 8

USA 11, 23
USSR 22, 23

Venezuela 23

zinc 21, 28

Picture acknowledgements

The publishers would like to thank the following for allowing their photographs to be reproduced in this book: British Steel plc *title page*, 14, 17; Cephas Picture Library *cover* (top), 4 (Mick Rock), 5 (Nigel Blythe), 21 top (Norman Van Abbe), bottom (W Geiersperger); Mary Evans Picture Library 9; Eye Ubiquitous 6 (Paul Seheult), 20 (Paul Seheult); Hutchison Library *cover* (bottom); J Allan Cash Ltd 7, 8, 10, 11, 12, 18, 25; Wayland Picture Library 24; Zefa Picture Library 22, 26, 27. Artwork is by Jenny Hughes.